THE ALL-TIME

★ ★ ★ ★ ★ ★ ★ ★ ★

ALL-STAR TEAM

★ ★ ★ ★

★ ★ ★ ★

RICHARD J. BRENNER

★ ★ ★ ★ ★ ★ ★ ★ ★

EAST END PUBLISHING, LTD.
MILLER PLACE, NEW YORK

This book is dedicated to all people who are courageously and compassionately working to se
cure universal human rights and attempting to eliminate all forms of bigotry, whether it is base
on skin color, creed, country of origin, or gender orientation.

In that spirit, I specifically dedicate this book to Ai Weiwei, a renowned artist who has bee
imprisoned in China because of his advocacy of human rights.

My sincere thanks to Scholastic Book Fairs, for their continued support, and to some of the people who assist
in the creation of this book, including Sarah Becker, Temeka Muse, Izabela Belcastro, and Erin Molta .

Book design: Izabela Belcastro   **Copy editor:** Erin Molta

Photo Credits: The image of Tony Gonzalez was taken by **Derick Hingle** and supplied by Icon/SMI. Getty Im-
ages supplied the remaining photographs. The individual photographers' names appear in bold, next to the names
the players whose image they took, as per the following: Joe Montana * **George Rose**; Jim Brown * **Tony Tomsi**
Jerry Rice * **Otto Greule Jr**; Anthony Muñoz * **Peter Brouillet**; Joe Greene * **Vernon Biever**; Ray Lewis * **Al
Messerschmidt**; Deion Sanders * **Brian Bahr**; Ronnie Lott * **Michael Zagaris**; Adam Vinatieri * **Kevin Terrel**

ISBN: 0-943403-79-0 * 978-0-943403-79-3

Published by EAST END PUBLISHING, LTD.
18 Harbor Beach Road
Miller Place, NY 11764

Printed in the United States of America by Universal Printing Co.

Richard J. Brenner, America's best-selling sportswriter, has written nearly 100 exciting sports
titles. For details on how to order a small sampling of those books, see the last page of this
book or send an email to: rjbrenner1@gmail.com.

Mr. Brenner is also available to speak at schools and other venues. For details, including fees
you may e-mail him directly at: rjbrenner1@gmail.com, or write to him c/o EEP, 18 Harbor
Beach Road, Miller Place, NY 11764.

★ ★ ★

AUTHOR'S MESSAGE: For many years, Native American groups have been appealing to sports teams not
use logos and names, such as Redskins, that many people find offensive. Out of respect for, and in support o
those appeals, I have chosen not to use such names in this book.

INTRODUCTION

I should confess that it's not possible to create a definitive all-time all-star team. It's difficult enough to choose a reasonably accurate annual all-star squad and even more so to select an all-decade team; but comparing athletes from multiple generations, who played against different competition, and under constantly evolving sets of rules, is more art than science. It should be considered a rough approximation, rather than a concrete certainty.

You may wonder, then, why I wrote this book. The answer is quite simple: I've always enjoyed provoking discussions, and I think that human beings have a natural urge to compare and rank performances and performers. That's true whether the subject is rap artists or presidents, movie stars or super heroes. Who do you dig more, Batman or The Hulk? Does Eminem top your play list, or is it Lil Wayne or Ludacris or someone else?

The urge to compare and rank players prompts sports fans to spend thousands of hours a week on blogs and radio call-in shows, tiresomely trying, for example, to make the case that Tom Brady is a better quarterback than Peyton Manning, or that Chris Johnson is a better running back than Adrian Peterson. But after all the shouting subsides, those discussions really turn on opinions—only some of which are informed—and suggestive stats, not absolute facts. There are simply too many variables to consider in attempting to evaluate an individual player in a team sport as intricate as football. It's a game in which individual performances have to be teased out of a series of complex patterns and subtle movements that often happen faster than the human eye can actually register them.

That's why, in fact, instant replay and slow motion cameras have changed our understanding of the game, and it's also why coaches and players spend so much time in the film room, dissecting what happened on the field and discovering things they couldn't decipher while standing on the sideline or being involved in the play.

Likewise, raw statistics aren't conclusive when comparing players, even in a given year, let alone across decades, since an individual's stats are reflective not only of his unique talents, but also of the relative quality of his teammates and the teams that they played against. How, for example, can we realistically judge the merits of two similarly gifted quarterbacks when one plays behind a leaky offensive line, with mediocre receivers, while the other one plays behind a steadfast line and throws to a trio of Pro Bowl-level receivers? And how do we calculate the competitive differences between these two hypothetical quarterbacks if one plays his home games in an outdoor stadium, where weather conditions can dictate outcomes of games, and the other one plays at least half of his games in a climate-controlled dome, where wind, rain, and snow are abstractions rather than contentious realities?

So, now that I've made the case for the impossibility of my task, here's my selection of football immortals. I hope that you enjoy reading about some of your favorite players and learning about others who you may never have heard of.

QUARTERBACK

Quarterback is, without question, the most important and the most difficult position to master. The ability to play the position at the highest level requires an astonishing amount of physical skill, mental acuity, and emotional steadiness.

"Playing quarterback in the NFL is so tough it is almost impossible," noted Hall of Fame coach Paul Brown. "The basic reason is that there is a degree of excellence required that is so high it is virtually unimaginable to outsiders."

Physically, a quarterback has to have quick feet, to avoid pass rushes; be skilled at ball handling and faking; have a strong arm; a quick release; and, most essentially, be able throw a football to a moving target with pinpoint accuracy. He has to be intelligent enough to learn and memorize hundreds of different plays, and to know what each of his teammates will do on each of them. He also needs to be able to recognize defensive schemes and, in the blink of an eye, change a play at the line of scrimmage.

What ultimately stamps a quarterback with greatness, however, is the ability to play his best when the games mean the most.

"You can't win championships without a great quarterback," declared Buddy Parker, who coached Detroit to two titles in the 1950s, when the Lions knew how to roar. "As far as a title is concerned, you might as well stay at home if you don't have a big guy at that spot. The quarterback who can win championships is the most precious commodity in pro football."

JOE MONTANA (1979-1994)

"There have been and will continue to be NFL quarterbacks with better arms and greater running ability than Joe Montana had," said Randy Cross, a former San Francisco 49er teammate of Montana. "But if you have to score a touchdown to win a championship, the only guy you want is Joe Montana."

Montana began displaying his gift for late game heroics as a Pennsylvania prep school star, and he continued his theatrics at Notre Dame, where he quarterbacked the Fighting Irish to the 1977 national championship and earned the nickname the Comeback Kid. His most dramatic performance came in his final collegiate contest, the 1979 Cotton Bowl, against the Houston Cougars. Playing on a frozen, wind-whipped field and with only 7:37 left in the game, Montana rallied the Irish from a 34-12 deficit to a 35-34 triumph.

"When the pressure is on," as Hall of Fame quarterback Roger Staubach would later say, "Joe Montana is as good as anyone who has ever played the game."

Montana, who was selected in the third round of the 1979 draft by the 49ers, became the full-time starter in 1981, and promptly showed the NFL what Montana Magic was about. First, he broke the hearts of the Dallas Cowboys in the NFC title game by capping a late-game scoring drive with a game-winning touchdown pass. He followed that performance with more high drama against the Cincinnati Bengals in Super Bowl XVI, when he directed another late game-winning drive, a 92-yard record-setting piece of quarterbacking artistry. His performance earned him the first of his three Super Bowl MVP awards, and high praise from his demanding coach, Bill Walsh.

★ Joe Montana ★
QUARTERBACK

"He may have the greatest football instincts I have ever seen," said Walsh.

Three years later, the 49ers were back in the Super Bowl, but the media attention was focused on the opposing quarterback, Dan Marino. The Miami Dolphins' second-year star had electrified the league by setting records for touchdown passes and passing yardage. Hall of Fame quarterback Joe Namath acknowledged Marino's passing ability, but when he was asked to pick a winner, he placed his faith in Montana.

"Marino is the best passer I've ever seen," said Namath. "But if I have to win one game, I'll go with Montana."

Montana rewarded that conviction with a record-setting performance that sparked the 49ers to a lopsided win. Four years later, the Niners trailed the Bengals in Super Bowl XXIII, with only 3:10 remaining in the game, and the ball at their own eight-yard line. But Montana marched the team relentlessly down the field, as he completed eight of nine pass attempts, including the game-winning strike with only 34 clicks left on the clock. The following year, Montana made it look easy by throwing for five touchdowns and earning his third Super Bowl MVP award, as the Niners nailed the Denver Broncos in Super Bowl XXIV.

In his four Super Bowl appearances, when it counted the most, Montana was at his most magical, completing 68 percent of his attempts, while passing for 1,142 yards, 11 touchdowns, and zero interceptions.

"When the game is on the line, and you need someone to go in there and win it right now, I would rather have Joe Montana as my quarterback than anyone else who has ever played the game," declared Bill Walsh. "No one has been able to win with all the chips down like Joe."

HONORABLE MENTIONS

★

TOM BRADY (2000-)

He's a two-time Super Bowl MVP, and the only quarterback to lead game-winning drive in the fourth quarter of three Super Bowls.

★

JOHNNY UNITAS (1956-1973)

He piloted the Baltimore Colts to a trio of championships, including the 1958 OT win over the New York Giants, dubbed by many football historians as the Greatest Game Ever Played.

★

PEYTON MANNING (1998-)

He's the only NFL player to win four MVP awards, and is, arguably, the best passer ever. If he stays healthy, he will own all the major career records.

★

DAN MARINO (1983-1999)

He held all the major career passing records when he retired, in 1999, and held them until Brett Favre eclipsed his marks a decade later.

★

OTTO GRAHAM (1946-1955)

He led the Cleveland Browns into a championship game in every season of his 10-year career, and earned seven titles.

★

JOHN ELWAY (1983-1998)

He propelled the Denver Broncos to three Super Bowl appearances, including wins in SB XXXII and XXXIII, the final game of his NFL career.

★

TERRY BRADSHAW (1970-1983)

He's the only quarterback other than Montana to lead a team, the Pittsburg Steelers, to four Super Bowls wins.

RUNNING BACK

"I was never taught to do what I did," said Hall of Fame running back Red Grange, whose electrifying play helped to popularize the NFL in the 1920s. "And I know that I couldn't teach anyone else how to run."

Although the *Galloping Ghost* may have overstated the case, his essential point rings true: which is that, unlike quarterbacks, great running backs rely on instinct, not analysis. Grange, of course, played at a time when offensive and defensive schemes weren't nearly as complicated as they are today; and when the forward pass was a rarity, rather than a major factor in the game.

But whatever the era, great running backs all need to possess speed, quickness, strength, and great field vision. They also need to have the ability to hold on to the ball when being hammered; and have the willingness to block, when asked to do so, and, in the modern game, to be a sure-handed receiver.

Some running backs have speed to the outside, but aren't effective running inside, while others can run effectively only in the narrow range between their offensive tackles. But the great ones can do it all. They have the power to break tackles, and can run to daylight through the thinnest crack; the elusiveness to make tacklers miss them, and the speed to take to the house. The great ones aren't just confident about their ability; they're arrogant about it.

"I feel that I can always beat my man one-on-one," said Gayle Sayers, when he was rushing his way to the Hall of Fame. "And, two-on-one, I can beat them 75 percent of the time."

Author's note: While most teams today employ offensives that use a single back and three wide receivers, I've opted to focus on the top-two players at each of those positions.

JIM BROWN (1957-1965)

One of the few selections in this book that are almost beyond reasonable debate is the choice of Jim Brown as the top running back in NFL history.

"Jim Brown was not only the greatest running back of all time, but one of the four or five finest professional football players of all time," declared Hall of Fame coach George Allen. "He was a very big man, who combined size, speed, strength, and elusiveness better than any other runner pro football ever has."

Brown became the best running back in the NFL during his first season with the Cleveland Browns, when he led the league rushing, and he was the best runner in his final season, when he again led the league in rushing, for the eighth time in his incredible nine-year career.

He could bowl over linebackers and outrun defensive backs, and he was a durable player, who led the league in rushing attempts seven times, but never missed a game.

Brown was a virtual force of nature, who raged across gridirons with an iron-willed determination. By the time he retired, he had rewritten the record book, setting new marks for, among other things, single-game, single-season and career rushing-yards, and touchdowns scored. Although many of his records have been eclipsed by backs whom have played more games per-season and more seasons than he did, Brown is still tops in yards-per-carry, at 5.2, and remains the only running back to have averaged more than 100 rushing-yards per game.

"Jim Brown was the greatest I ever saw or played against," said Hall of Fame linebacker Chuck Bednarik. *"No one else was even close."*

★ JIM BROWN ★
RUNNING BACK

WALTER PAYTON (1975-1987)

Although he played behind some medio-re offensive lines early in his career with the Chicago Bears, Walter Payton was never any-thing less than excellent. He was the ultimate professional, a hard-nosed player, who led the league in rushing attempts four times and who missed only one game in his 13-year career. By the time he retired, after the 1987 season, Payton held a host of NFL career records, in-cluding most rushing yards (16,726) and most yards from scrimmage (21,264). Although those records have since been erased, Payton's impact remains indelible.

"He was the best running back that I ever saw," declared Hall of Fame coach John Mad-den.

He was not only a great runner, he was also an excellent pass receiver and a fero-cious blocker, who listed hitting, not scor-ing touchdowns, as his biggest thrill on a football field.

"When a safety or a linebacker blitzes, I peel back, and just as he's ready to get to the quarterback," explained Payton, I turn his lights out."

Payton played the game all-out on every play, using his body as a battering ram. Even along the sideline, where most other backs tiptoe out of bounds to avoid a hit, Peyton would lower his shoulder and explode into a would-be tackler.

"Walter had all the skills and the ultimate heart, a mix that can take a man anywhere," said Jim Brown. "His energy and athleticism and determination were awesome. He had a dynamic first step. He had striking power. Walter weighed about 195 pounds, but struck like 220."

HONORABLE MENTIONS

★

BARRY SANDERS (1989-1998)

Averaged more than 1,500 rushing yards during his spectacular 10-year NFL career, topped by his 2,053 yards in 1997, the second-highest single-season total ever.

★

MARSHALL FAULK (1994-2005)

A three-time Offensive Player of the Year and a Super Bowl MVP, Faulk became the second running back to amass 1,000 yards of rushing and receiving in the same season.

★

ERIC DICKERSON (1983-1993)

He rushed for 10,000 yards faster than any other player (91 games), and set the single-sea-son rushing record in 1984, with 2,105 yards.

★

O.J. SIMPSON (1969-1979)

The first player to rush for more than 2,000 yards in a season, Simpson won four rushing titles playing for mostly me-diocre teams.

★

EMMITT SMITH (1990-2004)

Set the NFL career marks for rushing yards (18,355) and rushing touchdowns (164), while winning four rushing titles and three Super Bowls.

★

LADAINIAN TOMLINSON (2001-)

Set the single-season record for touchdowns (31) scored and rushing touchdowns (28), and has averaged more than 1,300 rushing yards with just under 60 receptions per season.

★

GAYLE SAYERS (1965-1971)

"Sayers may have been the purest natural runner I've ever seen," said Hall of Fame coach Vince Lombardi. "He was our single greatest defensive challenge."

WIDE RECEIVER

Although speed is always an asset on the gridiron, it isn't the essential weapon in the arsenal of a great receiver. If it were, NFL rosters would be filled with track stars; but Bob Hayes is the only wide receiver ever to win an Olympic gold medal as a sprinter, and to also be enshrined into the Pro Football Hall of Fame.

Some of the all-time greats, such as Raymond Berry, Johnny Unitas' favorite target, and Steve Largent, a record-setting wide-out for the Seattle Seahawks, ran more like Clydesdales than greyhounds. What they lacked in speed, however, they more than made up for with outstanding moves.

"The secret isn't pure speed, but how you make your cut," explained Jackie Smith, a Hall of Fame receiver. "That's what separates the good receivers from the ordinary ones, making the cut in full stride, so that a defensive back can't adjust. And you have to be able to set him up, so that he's looking for one move, while you actually do a different one. That's how you beat a defensive back."

The great ones also have Velcro-like hands for catching and holding on to the ball when they're hit, an ability to gain yardage after the catch, and steely determination and total concentration.

"When a ball is thrown in my direction, I know it's my ball; it doesn't belong to the defensive back or to the ground," said former New York Jets wide receiver George Sauer. "I follow the ball into my hands with such con-centration that I can see the grain of leather. I can even see the words printed on the ball."

JERRY RICE (1985-2004)

People say that records are meant to be broken, but the numbers that Jerry Rice reached are so extraordinary, they may never even be approached, let alone bettered. Just a most discussions about the best running back start with Jim Brown, Rice always leads the pack when the talk turns to wide receivers.

"Jerry Rice is probably the only guy at a position that is clearly, clearly the best ever at his position," said Keyshawn Johnson, a football analyst and former Pro Bowl receive "You could debate anybody, but you can't debate him."

Rice staked his claim to greatness in his initial season in the NFL, when he was name the NFC Rookie of the Year and startled vet-eran players with his level of ability.

"The first time I ever saw him, he was best I had ever seen, and I learned to turn on the television at an early age," said Dwight Clark, a former teammate and fellow wide receiver. "Jerry is like a Michael Jordan, a Joe Montana. He's a step above the field."

Although Rice was blessed with great abil ity, the secret to his success was his legendary work ethic.

"Everyone sees what happens on Sunday,' explained Rice. "But it's what you did the res of the week that determines what happens in the game."

Rice's 20-year record-setting career was a almost unbroken reel of highlight tape, dur-ing which he won three Super Bowl rings and a Super Bowl MVP award, and was named to the NFL Team of the Decade for the 1980s and the 1990s.

"I've seen them all," said Steve Sabol, the late president of NFL Films, "and Rice is the greatest receiver ever to play the game."

★ JERRY RICE ★
WIDE RECEIVER

DON HUTSON (1935-1945)

During his 11 seasons with the Green Bay Packers, Don Hutson set the standard by which all other receivers have been judged. In his initial start, in 1935, he pulled in his first reception and galloped 83 yards to score the game's only touchdown. In his final season, he scored four touchdowns in a single quarter and led the league in receiving for the eighth time. Hutson took the NFL by storm, shook it up, and forever changed the way football would be played.

When he came into the league, defenses dominated games. Teams averaged less than five completions and 70-yards passing per game. Fortunately for Hutson, the Packers had a quality quarterback, Arnie Herber, and an innovative coach, Curly Lambeau. Together, the trio essentially invented the modern passing game.

It was Hutson who introduced route running and feinting into the receiving position, and who caused defenses to employ double-and-triple teams to try to stop him.

"Hutson was the only man I ever saw," recalled Greasy Neale, an opposing coach, "who could feint in three different directions at the same time."

Hutson, who was a two-time MVP, created and dominated his position more thoroughly than any other player ever had. In 1942, playing in an 11-game season, he snared 17 touchdown passes, shattering the single-season record of nine; and he also became the first player to exceed 1,000 yards in receptions.

By the time he retired, in 1945, his name was stamped all over the record book. And the fact that some of his records are still standing—including most seasons leading the league in receptions (8), reception yardage (7), and touchdown receptions (9)—testifies to what a towering figure he remains today.

HONORABLE MENTIONS

★

RANDY MOSS (1998-)

The most gifted and dangerous receiver of his generation, Moss holds the single-season record for receiving touchdowns (23) which he set in 2007.

★

MICHAEL IRVIN (1988-1999)

A member of the NFL's All-Decade Team of the 1990s, Irvin was the premiere receiver on Dallas Cowboys teams that won three Super Bowls.

★

MARVIN HARRISON (1996-2008)

A member of the NFL's All-Decade Team of the 2000s, Harrison averaged 84.8 receptions per season, and set the single-season record for receptions with 143, in 2002.

★

PAUL WARFIELD (1964-1974, 1976-197

Although Warfield played on teams tha tended to run much more than they passed, he was an eight-time Pro Bowl selection and averaged 20.1 yard per catch for his career.

★

CHARLIE TAYLOR (1964-1975, 1977)

Switched to receiver two seasons after win ning the NFL Rookie of the Year award as a running back, Taylor registered 649 receptior good for 9,110 yards and 79 touchdowns.

★

CRIS CARTER (1987-2002)

Only one of six players in NFL history with 1,000 or more receptions, Carter tallied 130 touchdown catches and was a member o the NFL All-Decade Team of the 1990s.

★

TERRELL OWENS (1996-)

A member of the NFL's All-Decade Team of the 2000s, Owens stands second all-time in receiving yards, and is tied for second in receiving touchdow

TIGHT END

The tight end, a hybrid position that fuses blocker with a receiver, didn't come into be-g until the mid-20th century. Over the years, e position has evolved from one in which e ability to block was most highly valued, to ne in which coaches want athletes to be ad-ot at both receiving and blocking, especially n running plays.

Pete Pihos, who played for the Philadel-nia Eagles, was the first notable to play the osition, and he was so good that he led the ague in receptions for three straight seasons. ver the years, coaches have continued to evelop the position by exploiting the abili-es of bigger and faster athletes. Where once, oaches were content to use tight ends as ort-to medium-range receivers, now they ok for players, like Tony Gonzalez and An-nio Gates, who can run deep patterns and etch the field.

The position has become so important modern offenses, that teams often ploy schemes that use two tight ends. In me offensive packages, the tight end lines in the backfield, where he will usually act a lead blocker for the tailback. In that role, , essentially, becomes a fullback, and is usu-y designated as the H-Back.

"The tight end is, without a doubt, one of r most complex positions, simply because what we ask them to do," said Atlanta Fal-ns head coach Mike Smith. "We need them be very multiple. We not only want them to e up at the tight end position, we also ask em to shift into the backfield and lineup as a llback."

TONY GONZALEZ (1997-)

Unlike most of the other all-time all-stars, Tony Gonzalez, a first round draft pick of the Kansas City Chiefs, was not an immediate impact player in the NFL. His slow start cer-tainly wasn't due to a lack of effort or enthu-siasm, since he hit the ground running in his first mini-camp with the team.

"It all goes pretty fast here," he noticed, speaking about the speed of NFL players. "But that's okay; I don't do anything in sec-ond gear; I go straight to fifth gear. And I'm anxious to see how good I really am."

During his rookie season, Gonzalez caught 33 passes in a back-up role. The following year, he cracked the starting line-up and upped his receptions total to 59, a team record for a tight end. On the surface, it seemed as if he had made good progress, but a look beneath the waterline revealed that Gonzalez had also dropped 14 passes. Those miscues frustrated him and also caused some self-doubt to cloud his mind.

"I'd worked so hard preparing for the sea-son," he explained. "I'd put in so many hours in the weight room and out on the field, and I didn't have anything to show for it."

That whiff of failure provoked painful childhood memories of his three-year stint in a Pop Warner Football League.

"I was awful, and I hated it," recalled Gon-zalez. "I was big, but I was a pudding; every-body pushed me around."

Instead of continuing to brood about his drops, Gonzalez spent the off-season reading motivational books to learn how he could let go of his mistakes and hold onto his temper.

"I discovered that you have to train your-self to have amnesia in this business," said Gonzalez. "When you drop a ball or make another kind of mistake, you have to block it out and go on to the next play."

Gonzalez showed just how much he had learned during the 1999 season, when he topped all NFL tight ends with 76 receptions and 849 receiving yards. In case anyone thought that he had reached his ceiling, Gonzalez laid down a marker.

"I can do a whole lot better," vowed Gonzalez, whose performance had earned him his first Pro Bowl appearance. "If people think this is good, just wait; there's more to come."

If anything, Gonzalez's promise of even better days to come turned into an understatement, as he has gone on to become a perennial Pro Bowl selection and the tight end on the NFL 2000s Team of the Decade. Statistically, there isn't a tight end who even compares to Gonzalez—who holds all the major career receiving records for a tight end, including receptions, receiving yards, and touchdowns.

"I don't like second place," said Gonzalez. "I'm out there trying to win everything."

"There's nobody who can catch a ball or adjust to a ball in the air like Tony can, probably not even wide receivers," said Dick Vermeil, who was Gonzalez's head coach for five years. "I tell my quarterback to throw it to Tony even when he's covered, because he has the advantage over any receiver."

After his first sluggish steps in the NFL, Gonzalez moved on to the fast track, which one day, he'll ride all the way to Canton.

"Tony Gonzalez is on his way to the Hall of Fame," said coach Mike Smith, the head coach of the Atlanta Falcons, the team to which Gonzalez was traded in 2009. "He's the greatest tight end in the history of the game."

HONORABLE MENTIONS

★

MIKE DITKA (1961-1972)

A five-time Pro Bowl selection, *Iron Mike* was a fine receiver, a fierce blocker, and the first tight end inducted into the Hall of Fame.

★

SHANNON SHARPE (1990-2003)

The seventh-round draft pick went to eight Pro Bowls, won three Super Bowl rings, and held all the major receiving records for the position when he retired.

★

KELLEN WINSLOW (1979-1987)

A five-time Pro Bowl choice, despite an injury-marred career, Winslow was the best deep-ball tight end, ever.

★

DAVE CASPER (1974-1984)

One of the best blockers ever to play the position, *The Ghost* was also a sure-handed receiver, and a five-time Pro Bowler.

★

ANTONIO GATES (2003-)

The seven-time Pro Bowler joined Tony Gonzalez as one of two tight ends chosen for the NFL's 2000s All-Decade Team.

★

JASON WITTEN (2004-)

The seven-time Pro Bowl pick has more receptions and receiving yards than any other tight end in Dallas Cowboys history.

★

JOHN MACKEY (1963-1972)

The five-time Pro Bowler introduced speed to the position, averaging 20.7 yards-per-catch as a rookie. He was the second tight end to be inducted into the Hall of Fame.

TONY GONZALEZ ★

TIGHT END

OFFENSIVE LINEMEN

Although offensive linemen rarely get any glory or attention, except when they're flagged for a penalty, they're the cogs that allow the machine to run. If the center, guards, and tackles don't do their jobs, the offense grinds to a halt. What's more, they need to carry out their individual assignments in precise coordination with their linemates, like a well-tuned engine.

The great ones are cat-quick and strong. They have the quickness to pull out and lead sweeps, and they have the strength to execute straight-ahead blocks and hold off defensive linemen and linebackers on passing plays.

CENTER
MEL HEIN (1931-1945)

Mel Hein was an incredible athlete, who played two-way football for 60 minutes a game during his 15-year career with the New York Giants, without ever missing a game.

Hein was such a dominant performer that he was named All-Pro for eight consecutive seasons, including 1938, when he became the only interior lineman ever named the NFL's MVP. He was a team leader and the captain of the Giants for ten seasons, a time span in which they won seven divisional titles and a pair of NFL championships. And he was also an innovator who developed many of the hiking and blocking techniques that are still used today.

It took a special type of person to excel at the center position in Hein's time, when every snap involved a deep snap to a tailback, and a defensive lineman in his face. Hein was that type of person—in every game, for 15 years.

Author note: Due to space limitations, this book will feature only one guard and one tackle in the main section.

TACKLE
ANTHONY MUÑOZ (1980-1992)

As the 1980 draft approached, NFL talent scouts flocked to the University of Southern California to check out Anthony Muñoz. Although a knee injury had sidelined him for most of his senior season, he had impressed the scouts with his attitude and his determination.

"He's everything you want in a pro football player," said one NFL personnel director. "A hard worker with a marvelous, likable personality."

The Cincinnati Bengals head coach at the time, Forrest Gregg, trekked out to California to personally work out Muñoz. Afterwards, Gregg, who is Hall of Fame tackle himself, raved about what he had seen.

"We've got to have this guy," declared Gregg, who selected Muñoz with the third pick of the draft. "He's a rare specimen. He moves better than any big man I've ever seen."

Muñoz was so good so quickly that he was named the NFL Offensive Lineman of the Year in 1981, the first of three times that he would win the award.

Defensive ends grew old attempting to get around Muñoz to register a sack, and he was also a fabulous run-blocker, who helped Bengals' tailbacks pile up huge gobs of yardage.

"You watch films on Monday, and it's like, before I get hit, I'm five yards downfield because he creates such a large hole for me to run through," said one of those backs, Ickey Woods.

Muñoz, who was an All-Pro for 11 consecutive seasons, impressed everyone who ever saw him play, including George Allen, a veteran coach who had seen most of the all-time greats.

"He looks," noted Allen, "like one of the Immortals."

★ ANTHONY MUÑOZ ★
OFFENSIVE TACKLE

GUARD
GENE UPSHAW (1967-1981)

The Oakland Raiders installed Gene Upshaw at left guard in his rookie season, and he played the position with distinction for fifteen years. During that time, he was nearly indestructible, playing in all but one of the Raiders' 308 contests, including pre- and-post-season games.

Upshaw was big and strong, intelligent, and dedicated to perfecting his craft. And he wasn't just quick; he was fast. His favorite play was pulling out and leading the Raiders' running backs on the outside sweeps that the team loved to run.

"That's my play," said Upshaw, whose blocking helped lead the Silver and Black to a pair of Super Bowl wins. "A wide receiver wants to catch a long touchdown pass. A defensive tackle wants to break through and sack the quarterback. I get my satisfaction from leading those sweeps. That's when it comes down to just me and the defensive back. If I get him clean, we're going to make a big gain. If I miss him, we don't get a yard."

Upshaw got his man so often that he was generally recognized as the best run-blocking guard ever. And while no offensive lineman enjoys receiving the punishment they absorb while protecting their quarterback, he took pride in becoming excellent at that role, too.

"I didn't have as much fun pass blocking, but I did get satisfaction from it," he noted. "That's where we separate the men from the boys. It takes a hell of a man to stand in there and take those roundhouse clubs to the head and the butting with the helmets."

"If there was a better guard," said John Madden, "I never saw him."

HONORABLE MENTIONS
★

JIM OTTO C (1960-1974)
An All-League performer for 12 consecut seasons for the Oakland Raiders, Otto playec six title games, including Super Bowl II.

CLYDE TURNER C (1940-1952)
Like Mel Hein, *Bulldog Turner* was a gif 60-minute player, who was named to the NF Team of the Decade for the 1940s.

MIKE WEBSTER C (1974-1990)
An All-Pro for seven seasons and the Pittsburgh Steelers offensive captain for nine years, Webster helped the Steelers win four Super Bow

RUSS GRIMM G (1981-1991)
Was a standout *Hog*, the offensive line t powered Washington to back-to-back Super Bowl appearances.

JOHN HANNAH G (1973-1985)
"He developed into as good a guard as there ever was in the NFL," said John Madden. "Maybe the best ever."

JIM PARKER G (1957-1967)
He was an All-Pro selection for eight stra years, the first four as the Baltimore Colts le tackle, the final four as their left guard.

FORREST GREGG T (1956, 1958-197
"Forrest Gregg is, quite simply, the fine football player I've ever coached," said Vi Lombardi, the legendary coach of the Gree Bay Packers.

ROOSEVELT BROWN T (1953-1965
An obscure 27th-round draft pick, Brow was an All-Pro for eight consecutive seasor for the New York Giants.

DEFENSIVE LINEMEN

Just as offense line play is about blocking and execution, the name of the game on the defensive side of the *Pit* is penetration and hitting. Usually, the team that wins the battle in the trenches between the two lines will also win the game.

For the defensive line, controlling the line of scrimmage means closing down the running lanes, gaining penetration, and pressuring the quarterback. Generally, defensive ends are better at rushing the passer than they are at stopping the run, just as tackles are, usually, more adept at stopping the run than they are at rushing the quarterback. Their relative abilities are a matter of both design and selection, because the overall plans of defenses dictate their personnel decisions.

Defenses are designed, for the most part, to have their pass rush come from the outside because there's less congestion on the wings than in the center of the field. The reason that they tend to put their best run-stoppers at tackle is because most offenses would prefer to pound the ball up the middle, guided as they are by the principle that a straight line is the shortest distance between two points—i.e., the line of scrimmage and the first down marker.

Of course, great linemen make plays all over the field, and they are so disruptive that they are effective even before the game begins. That's because offensive coordinators are forced to create game plans to defend against the threat of great linemen. Instead of formulating a positive game plan, the O.C. is put on the defensive before the opening kickoff.

Author note: Due to space limitations, this book will feature only one end and one tackle in the main section.

END
DAVID JONES (1961-1974)

Perhaps the best way to judge the quality of a player is to pay attention to the praise they receive from the Hall of Famers who played against them.

"I not only beat most pass rushers, I annihilated them," said Jim Parker. "I never mastered Jones, though. Nobody did. The most I did was break even. How many men do you think ever beat me? *Forget it*. But he did. Lots of times. And you knew he was never going to quit. He went at it as if his life depended upon it on every play."

Ironically, Jones, who was nicknamed *Deacon*, was such a low-rated prospect that he was hardly given a chance to make the Los Angeles Rams. But he used his exceptional speed, strength, and determination to not only make the squad, but to become a two-time NFL Defensive Player of the Year.

"I won't say that I wasn't scared at first," said Jones, who coined the word, *sack*, and made the play his calling card. "But there was no one going to scare me away."

In fact, it was Jones who wound up scaring offenses as few other defensive players ever have.

"He's the only defender who changes the tempo of the game," said John Brodie, an All-Pro quarterback of the day.

"He's one guy I will remember as long as I live," said Forrest Gregg. "Out of the hundreds and hundreds of good football players I've faced, the Deacon will stand out. No man I've faced had his quickness, his speed, or his moves. He could outrun any back we had."

TACKLE
JOE GREENE (1969-1981)

When the Pittsburgh Steelers hired Chuck Noll as their head coach in 1969, his first move was to select Joe Greene with the team's first-round draft pick. Noll thought that Greene, who was nicknamed *Mean Joe*, could become the keystone of a championship defense. Greene immediately began rewarding that faith by playing at a level that earned him the Defensive Rookie of the Year Award and the first of his 10 trips to the Pro Bowl.

Three years later, Greene won the first of his two Defensive Player of the Year awards. He clinched the prize with a dominating display in a game against the Houston Oilers that allowed the Steelers to win the AFC Central Division title. In a show for the ages, Greene registered five sacks against Houston quarterback Dan Pastorini, blocked a field goal attempt, and both caused and recovered a fumble that set up the game-winning field goal. The divisional title provided the Pittsburgh franchise with its first-ever championship.

"It was just an incredible performance," said Noll. "I've watched the film a dozen times and I still can't believe it."

Two years later, Greene fulfilled his coach's ultimate aspirations when he led the Steelers to victory in Super Bowl IX, something that he would do three more times in the span of five years.

"He's the best I've ever seen," declared Noll. "He set the standard for us. Physically, he had all the necessary attributes, but he also set the standard for attitude. There will never be another Joe Greene. Joe will always be something special."

HONORABLE MENTIONS
★

GINO MARCHETTI E (1952-1964, 196
"He had great moves and desire," said Deacon Jones, of the seven-time All-Pro. "H had it all. He was a complete package."

★

REGGIE WHITE E (1985-2000)
The Minister of Defense, was an unstopp ble force, a two-time Defensive Player of th Year, and the number two career sack leade

★

BRUCE SMITH E (1885-2003)
The league's all-time sack, with 200 qua terback drops, Smith was a two-time Defen sive Player of the Year and helped the Buffa Bills get to four Super Bowl appearances.

★

WILLIE DAVIS E (1958-1969)
An All-Pro for five seasons, he helped lead the Green Bay Packers to six titles, including a pair of Super Bow victories.

★

MICHAEL STRAHAN E (1993-2007)
The Defensive Player of the Year in 200 Strahan helped spark the New York Giants a win in Super Bowl XLII, and was selecte for the NFL 2000s All-Decade Team.

★

MERLIN OLSEN T (1962-1976)
A member of the NFL Team of the Deca for the 1960s, Olsen played in 14 consecuti Pro Bowl games and, for 10 years, formed great defensive duo with Deacon Jones.

★

ALAN PAGE T (1967-1981)
Won the first-ever Defensive Player of t Year award in 1971, the same year that he became the first defensive player ever to be named the league MVP.

★ JOE GREENE ★
DEFENSIVE TACKLE

LINEBACKER

If the name of the game on defense is hitting, then a linebacker must have created the rules of the game, because linebackers *love* to hit. Due to the way defenses are structured, with linebackers playing either behind the down linemen or in the gaps between them, they get a great deal of opportunities to deliver their own special brand of valentine.

Linebackers can, depending upon the play and their assignment, roam the entire field, from coast to coast and north to south, wrapping up tailbacks on running plays, and then, on passing plays, either dropping into coverage or blitzing the quarterback.

In addition to being strong enough to fight through the blocks of 300-pound linemen, great linebackers must have the speed to cover receivers, chase down running backs, or reach a quarterback in a matter of seconds. Perhaps most importantly, they must have a nose for the ball and razor-sharp football instincts, because they have only a fraction of a second to decide if the play is a run or a pass before they move into position. Linebackers don't have the time for conscious thought and analysis.

"We've got our keys to read, but if you stop to figure them out, you're dead," explained Larry Grantham, a former Pro Bowl linebacker with the New York Jets. "I'm looking at one man, but I'm really seeing five, and my legs move before my brain catches up. There's absolutely no waiting involved."

Author's note: Some teams use a three-man linebacking grouping, while others opt for four, employing two on the inside and a pair on the outside. This book will feature one inside and one outside linebacker in the main section.

RAY LEWIS (1996-)

Ray Lewis, the Baltimore Ravens' bone-crunching tackler, came into the NFL with a chip on his shoulder because he was only the fifth linebacker selected in the 1996 draft.

"My goal is to be the best middle linebacker," said Lewis. "When I'm done playing, I want people to say that Ray Lewis was the greatest of all time."

Lewis took a step toward his objective in his very first game, when he racked up nine tackles and an interception, and was named the AFC Defensive Player of the Week. And every stride he's taken since then has taken him closer to Canton and his ultimate goal.

In 2000, Lewis won the first of his two Defensive Player of the Year awards, when he anchored a record-setting Ravens defense.

Then, he capped that brilliant run by being named the MVP of Baltimore's Super Bowl victory over the New York Giants.

Although his list of personal accomplishments and awards is long and distinguished, Lewis' greatest achievement may be his role as team leader.

"He's the heart and soul of the team," said former Baltimore coach Brian Billick. "The most naturally dynamic leader I've ever been around."

During the 2010 season, Lewis, still going strong after 15 seasons in the league, was named to his 12th Pro Bowl team, and became only the second player in NFL history to record at least 30 sacks and 30 interceptions in career.

"He's still playing as well as any middle linebacker in football today," said Ravens coach John Harbaugh. "In my opinion, he's the greatest middle linebacker in the history the game."

RAY LEWIS
INSIDE LINEBACKER

LAWRENCE TAYLOR
(1981-1993)

The first time that Lawrence Taylor put on the pads at a New York Giants intrasquad scrimmage, he created such havoc that his teammates started referring to him as *Superman*. Seasoned veterans watched in awe as the rookie linebacker smashed through or ran around the players assigned to block him. In that single ten-minute drill, Taylor recorded four sacks and recovered a fumble, as he thoroughly outplayed everyone who lined up against him.

"He's either going to run around you or over you," said Phil Simms, the Giants quarterback. "With his quickness, he's full speed after two steps."

Taylor's impact on the NFL was immediate and monumental. With the speed of a tailback, the strength of an oak tree, and an intense desire to wreak mayhem, Taylor became the only player ever named the Rookie of the Year and the Defensive Player of the Year in the same season. Taylor would go on to become the only player to win the DPY award three times, and only the second defensive player ever to be named the league's MVP.

He not only won awards, he forced opponents into altering their offensive schemes, and he also helped transform the mediocre Giants into two-time Super Bowl champions. By the time he retired, Taylor was considered by many to be the greatest defensive player of all-time.

"Lawrence Taylor, defensively, has had as big an impact as any player I've ever seen," said John Madden. "He changed the way defense is played, the way pass-rushing is played, the way linebackers play, and the way that offenses block linebackers."

HONORABLE MENTIONS
★
CHUCK BEDNARIK (1949-1962)

"His defensive judgments were instinctiv the best," declared Tom Brookshire, a former teammate. "You couldn't teach *Concrete Charley* anything playing linebacker."

★
DERRICK BROOKS (1995-2008)

The outside linebacker for the Tampa Bay Buccaneers was named the 2002 NFL Defensive Player of the Year and was also named t the NFL 2000s All-Decade Team.

★
DICK BUTKUS (1965-1973)

"Butkus played in the era of the great middle linebackers, but I think that no man ever did it as well as he did," said Jim Brow "Butkus was the ultimate hitter."

★
JACK HAM (1971-1982)

"Of all the outside linebackers I coached against, he was the best," said Jo Madden. "He was never out of position."

★
TED HENDRICKS (1969-1983)

The Stork, an eight-time Pro Bowl selection at outside linebacker, helped his teams t reach seven AFC title games and four Super Bowls.

★
JACK LAMBERT (1974-1984)

A two-time NFL Defensive Player of the Year and eight-time All-Pro with the Pittsburgh Steelers, Lambert was the defensive keystone of the teams that won four Super Bowls.

★
MIKE SINGLETARY (1981-1992)

A two-time NFL Defensive Player of the Year.

DEFENSIVE BACKS

A defensive back has to be able to cover and tackle. Those are the two basic and overriding requirements of the position. In some schemes, the defensive backs cover a zone, which makes them responsible for covering receivers in a specific area of the field. But the ultimate measure of a defensive back is his ability to play the best receivers one-on-one and limit, if not entirely eliminate their productivity.

Obviously, a defensive back has to be both fast and quick to stay with whippet-like wide receivers. But they also need to be strong enough to fight through the blocks of offensive linemen and tight ends, and be willing and able to meet a hard-running tailback and drop him in his tracks.

Defensive backs need to be thick-skinned and to have short memories when it comes to failure. They can't allow a bad coverage or a missed tackle to turn into an avalanche of blown assignments.

"The thing to remember is that you're going to get beat," explained Hall of Fame cornerback Herb Adderly. "The question is, When you get beat, can you recover.'"

Statistics—interceptions, tackles, passes defended, and sacks—can offer a rough draft of a defensive back's effectiveness. But they don't automatically convey the entire picture, because some defensive backs are so outstanding that offenses won't even challenge them. So, while a great defensive back doesn't necessarily pile up huge numbers, he does something even more important —he narrows the field and limits an offense's options.

Author's note: Although teams will often use five or six defensive backs when passing plays are anticipated, the traditional lineup consists of two cornerbacks and a pair of safeties. Generally, the cornerbacks cover wide receivers, while the strong safety covers the tight end, and the free safety follows his nose to the ball.

WILLIE BROWN

Willie Brown came into pro football through the backdoor in 1963, as an undrafted free agent of the Houston Oilers. He made so light an impression, though, that they traded him to the Denver Broncos prior to the opening game of the season.

In his first start for Denver, a New York Jets receiver, Don Maynard, torched him for 159-yards and a trio of touchdown passes from Jets quarterback Joe Namath. Brown was burned so badly, the Broncos coaches almost called the fire marshal.

Instead of being destroyed by that experience, Brown used it as a springboard, and he became a devout student of game films, looking for every edge he could find.

"Every receiver has some kind of little move that tips off where he's going," noted Brown, "and if you study the film enough, you'll find out what it is."

He learned his lessons so well, that the following season he was selected for the All-AFL team. In a rematch against the Jets, Brown completely turned the tables on his tormentors by intercepting four passes and leading the Broncos to an upset win.

"He gives you nothing," said Namath, stating his frustration and his admiration. "If it's not a perfect pass, you can't complete it. He's the best."

After four seasons in Denver, Brown played another dozen years with the Oakland Raiders, where he became such a dominant cornerback that he earned his way through the front doors of the Hall of Fame.

"Willie didn't want to let anybody catch a pass," recalled former Raiders coach John Madden. "Not ever. Not even in practice. Not even in training camp."

Author's note: The AFL was a rival of the NFL from 1960 until 1969, when the leagues merged, and most of the AFL teams became the AFC, a conference within the NFL.

DEION SANDERS
(1989-2000, 2004-2005)

Most players entering the NFL, even the great ones, have to learn to adjust to the speed at which the game is played at that level. In the case of Deion Sanders, a first-round draft pick of the Atlanta Falcons, it was the league that had to try to adjust to his speed, which it never quite did. The first time he touched the ball in the NFL, Sanders brought Atlanta fans out of their seats by turning a punt into a 68-yard touchdown romp.

"He's the greatest athlete I've ever seen," said Ken Herock, the Falcons director of player personnel. "Deion can play wide receiver; he could play tailback. He can do anything."

Sanders did do pretty much everything on the gridiron, including returning punts and kickoffs, and even, for a time, playing wide receiver. *Prime Time* was such a spectacular punt returner that he was named to the All-Decade Team of the 1990s in that specialty. But it was as a cornerback, perhaps the best cover corner of all-time, that Sanders earned his way into the Hall of Fame.

In 1994, Sanders was named the Defensive Player of the Year while playing for the San Francisco 49ers and then, in the postseason, he helped lead the Niners to a win in Super Bowl XXIX.

"Everyone took his lead," said 49ers safety Merton Hanks. "Everyone's level of play went up."

The following year, Sanders signed with the Dallas Cowboys and helped lead them to a Super Bowl title, too.

"This guy is a great defensive back," said John Madden, who has coached some of the all-time greats. "He's a superstar."

HONORABLE MENTIONS

MEL BLOUNT (1967-1977)

A member of the NFL 75th Anniversary team and the 1975 Defensive Player of the Year, helped lead the Pittsburgh Steelers to four Super Bowl victories.

RON WOODSON (1987-2003)

A member of the NFL 75th Anniversary team and the 1993 Defensive Player of the Year, his 71 career interceptions ranks third all-time.

MIKE HAYNES (1976-1989)

A member of the NFL 75th Anniversary an a nine-time Pro Bowl selection, Haynes was also the Defensive Rookie of the Year in 1976.

CHAMP BAILEY (1999-)

Selected for 10 Pro Bowls, a record for cornerbacks, and the 2000s All-Decade Team, Bailey was the NFL Alumni Defensive Back Player of the Year in 2006.

DICK LANE (1952-1965)

Night Train holds the single-season record with 14 interceptions, and his 68-career picks rank fourth all-time

CHARLES WOODSON (1998-)

The Defensive Rookie of the Year in 1998 Woodson was named Defensive Player of the Year in 2009 and to the All-Decade Team of the 2000s.

HERB ADDERLEY (1961-1972)

A member of the All-Decade Team of the 1960s, Adderley helped the Green Bay Packers win the first two Super Bowl titles ever played and then helped the Dallas Cowboys win one.

★ DEION SANDERS ★
CORNERBACK

RONNIE LOTT (1981-1995)

During his 15 years in the NFL, Ronnie Lott was moved from corner back to strong safety, to free safety. But whichever position he played, he did so with distinction, and as well as anyone ever has.

"You have to set standards," explained Lott. "It's an attitude of playing the game the way it's supposed to be played. I don't want to just play a position. I want to make plays, *big* plays."

Lott began making big plays in his first season with the San Francisco 49ers, when he picked off seven passes and returned three of them for touchdowns. He finished as the runner-up behind New York Giants linebacker Lawrence Taylor in the voting for Defensive Rookie of the Year. But Lott led the 49ers defensive charge in the postseason, intercepting a pair of passes against the Giants in the opening round, and then delivering a lode of big hits in the Niners' win over the Cincinnati Bengals in Super Bowl XVI.

The year before Lott arrived in San Francisco, the 49ers had finished with a losing record and the third-worst pass defense in NFL history. During his ten-year stay with the franchise, the Niners won eight NFC Western Division titles and four Super Bowls. The timing was anything but coincidental.

Lott, who was selected for two All-Decade Teams and the 75th Anniversary Team, as well as the Hall of Fame, was a high-impact player and big game performer who left a lasting imprint all over the NFL.

"Ronnie Lott sets the tempo for that defense," said Hall of Famer Mike Ditka. "He's the finest free safety I've ever seen."

KEN HOUSTON (1967-1980)

As a low-round draft pick, Ken Houston was a long shot to make it out of his first training camp with the Houston Oilers. Although he had been known as the *Monster Man* for the way he leveled ball carriers as a linebacker in college, he was too light to play the position in the pros.

The Oilers staff realized, however, that he had the speed, the agility, and the hitting ability to be a strong safety. He quickly validated that decision by delivering the kind of high-performance games that became emblematic of his entire career.

In only his fifth game, Houston led an Oilers comeback by scoring a touchdown on a long run with a fumble recovery, and then the clincher on a 45-yard touchdown scamper with an intercepted pass.

After four seasons with the Oilers, Houston was traded to Washington, who gave up five veterans to obtain him. Although that was a hefty price to pay, George Allen, the Washington coach, never regretted the swap.

"Kenny Houston had that something extra," said Allen. "He was a terrific team man, totally unselfish, and a marvelous player who cared more about team victories than he did about personal glory."

Despite his lack of selfishness, Houston did win a bucketful of personal awards, including selection to 12 Pro Bowl squads and the NFL Team of the Decade for the 1970s. Later, as toppers to his improbable career, Houston was inducted into the Hall of Fame and was also named one of three safeties on the league's 75th anniversary team.

★ RONNIE LOTT ★
SAFETY

HONORABLE MENTIONS

⭐

EMLEN TUNNELL (1948-1961)

A nine-time Pro Bowl selection and a member of the All-Decade Team of the 1950s, Tunnell had 79 career interceptions.

⭐

LARRY WILSON (1960-1972)

A member of the All-Decade Team of the 1960s and 1970s, Wilson was also named to the league's 75th Anniversary All-Time Team

⭐

PAUL KRAUSE (1964-1979)

A ball-hawking defender, Krause was an eight-time Pro Bowl selection, and is the career interceptions leader, with 81.

⭐

BRIAN DAWKINS (1996-)

An eight-time Pro Bowl selection and a member of the 2000s All-Decade Team, Dawkins is a tremendous hitter and leader.

⭐

ED REED (2002-)

The 2004 Defensive Player of the Year, Reed is a seven-time Pro Bowler and a member of the 2000s All-Decade Team. He holds the record for the two longest interception returns.

⭐

TROY POLAMALU (2003-)

The 2010 Defensive Player of the Year and a member of the 2000s All-Decade Team, Polamalu has helped the Pittsburgh Steelers win two Super Bowls.

⭐

DARREN SHARPER (1997-)

A member of the 2000s All-Decade Team, Sharper's 63 career interceptions is the sixth-highest total ever. He also holds the single-season record for interception return yards.

PUNTERS

⭐

SAMMY BAUGH (1937-1952)

Sammy Baugh is not only the best punter of all-time, he may be the best football player ever. Baugh led the NFL in interceptions in 1943, and he was a three-time All-Pro as a single wing tailback and then as a quarterback. As a passer, *Slinging Sammy* did as much to create the modern passing game as Don Hutson did as a receiver. After all these years, he still holds the single-season record for punting average, 51.4 yards, and ranks fifth in career average.

⭐

YALE LARY (1952-1953, 1956-1964)

Like Sammy Baugh, Lary was a phenomenal athlete and a multi-positional player, who excelled as a defensive back and returner, as well as a punter. As a punter, he was good enough to lead the league in average yards-per-punts for three years, and while his career average was a couple of yards less than Baugh's, Lary punted the ball so high that he once had a string of six games and thirty-two punts without a return.

⭐

RAY GUY (1973-1986)

The only punter ever taken in the first round of the NFL draft, Guy's punting helped the Oakland and Los Angeles Raiders win three Super Bowl titles. He was selected for the 1970s All-Decade Team and the NFL's 75th Anniversary Team.

⭐

JEFF FEAGLES (1988-2009)

Holds the record for most punting yards and for placing the most punts inside the 20-yard line.

KICKERS

★

ADAM VINATIERI (1996-)

Generally considered to be the best clutch kicker ever, *Automatic Adam* has kicked game-winning field goals in a pair of Super Bowl Games for the New England Patriots. During the course of his career with the Pats and the Indianapolis Colts, he has played in five Super Bowls and won four rings. He was named to the 2000s All-Decade Team.

★

JAN STENERUD (1967-1985)

The only kicker in the Hall of Fame who did not play a second position, Stenerud was the kicker on the NFL's 75th anniversary All-Time team.

★

MORTEN ANDERSEN (1982-2007)

The career leader in points scored, the *Great Dane* is a seven-time pro Bowl selection, and was named to the All-Decade teams of the 1980s and the 1990s.

★

GARY ANDERSON (1982-2004)

A member of the All-Decade Team of the 1980s and 1990s, Anderson became the first kicker to record a perfect season, when he split the uprights on each of his 59 PATs and 35 field goal attempts in 1998.

★

LOU GROZA (1946-1959, 1961-1967)

An All-Pro offensive tackle as well as a kicker, his game-winning field goal with 30 seconds left in the NFL Championship Game allowed the Cleveland Browns to win the title.

★

GEORGE BLANDA (1949-1975)

He was a memorable performer as a kicker and quarterback at an age when some people are in rockers. Along with Stenerud and Groza, one of only three kickers in the Hall of Fame.

★ ADAM VINATIERI ★
KICKER

ORDER FORM

THE ALL-TIME ALL-STAR TEAM: This exciting, photo-filled book names football's all-time all-stars, position by position.
32 pages, 8 x 11. $5.99 U.S.

WORLD SERIES SHOWDOWNS: The special excitement of all the World Series, from 2000-2009, is brought to life in this photo-filled narrative.
48 pages, 8 x 11. $5.99 U.S.   _____

WORLDWIDE BASEBALL SUPERSTARS: 15 of baseball's best players, including Albert Pujols, Johan Santana, and Ichiro Suzuki, are profiled in a book that includes 29 pages of photographs.
48 pages, 8 x 10. $5.99 U.S.   _____

ALEX RODRIGUEZ * ALBERT PUJOLS: A dual-biography of baseball's two top superstars. The book includes 16 pages of action-packed color photographs.
144 pages, 5 x 8. $5.99 U.S.   _____

TONY ROMO * BEN ROETHLISBERGER: A dual-biography of two football superstars. The book includes 16 pages of action-packed color photographs.
144 pages, 5 x 8. $5.99 U.S.   _____

TOM BRADY * LADAINIAN TOMLINSON: A dual-biography of two of the NFL's top players. The book includes 16 pages of action-packed color photographs.
144 pages, 5 x 8. $5.99 U.S.   _____

BRETT FAVRE: An easy-to-read photo-filled biography of one of football's all-time greats. Written especially for younger children.
32 pages, 8 x 8. $4.50 U.S.   _____

MARK McGWIRE: An easy-to-read photo-filled biography of one of baseball's all-time greats.
32 pages, 8 x 8. $4.50 U.S.   _____

Total number of book(s) ordered   _____

Add $1.50 per book if you want book(s) autographed by author.   _____

TOTAL COST OF BOOKS   _____

TAX (NY state residents must add appropriate sales tax)   _____

Shipping charges (in the U.S.) $2.50 per book, up to a maximum of $12.50 on orders of 10 or fewer books.   _____

For international orders, email publisher for current terms.

TOTAL PAYMENT ENCLOSED: (All payments must be in U.S. currency; checks and money orders only; credit cards not accepted).   _____

(Please print clearly.)

NAME _____

ADDRESS _____

CITY _____STATE _____ZIP CODE_____

SEND PAYMENTS TO:

EAST END PUBLISHING, LTD.

18 Harbor Beach Road, Miller Place, NY 11764

Discounts are available on orders of 25 or more books. For details write or email: rjbrenner1@gmail.com

Terms are subject to change without notice.